The Little Book of Self-Discovery

Koren McGeever

Published in 2022

Copyright © Koren McGeever 2022

All rights reserved. No part of this publication may be reproduced, stored in a retrieval system, transmitted or utilised in any form by any means, electronic, mechanical, photocopying or recording or otherwise, without the prior permission of the copyright owner.

Koren McGeever has asserted her right to be identified as the author of this work in accordance with the Copyright, Designs and Patents Act 1988.

Acknowledgements

I would like to thank Thea Newcomb for sharing her fabulous expertise to show me how to create this book using Canva. You made a dream of mine come true. Also a massive thank you to my lovely friend Amy Beveridge for working her magic by editing this little book. I feel very grateful to you both.

Disclaimer

It is not intended or advised that this book be used as a replacement for professional counselling. The questions posed throughout this book are to encourage your own personal discovery and growth. It is your responsibility alone to only explore aspects of your life that you feel comfortable in doing so at this moment in time. The author assumes no responsibility for your actions.

UK-based mental health resources

Samaritans: 116 123 or e-mail jo@samaritans.org

SANE: 0300 304 7000 or visit www.sane.org.uk

SHOUT UK text support service: 85258

Hub of Hope: www.hubofhope.co.uk

If you are experiencing a mental health crisis which you feel requires immediate attention, please consider attending your nearest A&E department or calling 999.

Contents

Meet the author	6
Introduction	7
Perspective	11
Change	15
Happiness	18
Being Yourself	21
Making decisions	27
Self-worth	32
Relationships	36
Boundaries	42
Splits in self	46
Self-love	49
Final thoughts	54
References	55

Meet the Author

I am Koren, a Scotland-based registered person-centred counsellor and psychotherapist with the British Association for Counselling and Psychotherapy (BACP). I have always had a passion for supporting the needs of others and actively sought out opportunities to pursue this career path.

I studied BSc (Hons) Psychology at the University of Stirling, the COSCA counselling skills course at the University of Glasgow and lastly completed my MSc in Counselling and Psychotherapy at the University of Strathclyde.

I felt called to enter this career path and I find it such a blessing and a privilege to work with clients. My clients past and present never fail to inspire me. It is extremely rewarding for me to see clients feel empowered, and have realisations and make decisions that in turn transform their lives. I also am very inspired by the works of Carl Rogers, the founder of the person-centred counselling approach.

Counselling and psychotherapy can often leave clients feeling more in control of their lives, more content within themselves and optimistic about their future. It is my hope that through this personal development book written from a person-centred theory perspective, person-centred counselling will be more widely understood and people will be able to read the theory, apply it to their own life circumstances and gain a better understanding of themselves in the process.

Introduction

This little book is designed for you to take some time out your life to focus on something precious and important — YOU. You are at the centre of this book. Throughout this book, various personal development topics are discussed from a person-centred theory perspective. Person-centred therapists such as myself base their practice on this theory.

Carl Rogers (who is pictured on the top right-hand corner) was an American psychologist (Rogers,1967) and founder of the person-centred approach (Sanders, 2006). Rogers did not agree with 'labelling' clients with a diagnosis (Elkins, 2009). Instead, he believed in creating a model for development and growth as opposed to the medical model which pathologises individuals through diagnosis, treatment and cure (Cooper et al., 2013).

He developed the humanistic approach to therapy in the 1940s, originally naming it 'client-centred' therapy (Baker et al., 2012). This was done to move away from the psychotherapist being viewed as the expert, but instead viewing the client as the expert of their own life and putting them at the centre of the therapeutic process (Baker et al., 2012). He used this term to increase autonomy and the client's sense of personal responsibility (Cooper et al., 2013).

8

Rogers deliberately used the term 'client' as opposed to the word 'patient' (Cooper et al., 2013; Elkins, 2009), along with changing the name from client-centred to person-centred counselling in the 1960s (Baker et al., 2012). This was all done to further remove any clinical-sounding aspects to the approach (Baker et al., 2012)

Rogers believed that every individual has the internal resources needed to grow and develop (Cooper et al., 2013; Mearns et al., 2013). All the tools and resources you need are within you. It is just a case of unlocking them, and turning the correct lock combination to release the beauty of human experience in its truest, fullest form.

Therefore, by discussing personal development topics from a Rogerian person-centred theory perspective, my hope is that this little book aids your self-discovery, growth and potential healing and acceptance in order to move towards your ideal, true self.

I will refer to your 'true self' a lot throughout this book as this is a fundamental goal of the person-centred approach. Your 'true self' refers to your innermost personality and being — the self that feels most authentic to what and who you really are (Grice, 2007).

Sometimes our thoughts and feelings can get all tangled up together like a ball of string. It is my hope that by working through the 10 personal development topics offered — along with thought-provoking questions for deep introspective, reflective practice — this ball of string will slowly unravel, taking a little bit at a time to see what lies at the end of it.

The 10 personal development topics discussed are as follows:

- Perspective
- Change
- Happiness
- Being yourself
- Making decisions
- Self-worth
- Relationships
- Boundaries
- Splits in self
- Self-love

Through these topics a little light will be shone on various aspects of your life — focusing your attention not only on things you wish to change, but also praising the parts of yourself that you love and appreciate.

10

This book is not designed to be rushed through. Take the time to ponder over these topics and process what they bring up for you. Throughout this book, questions are offered for each topic, along with boxes to write in if you wish to do so. These are thought-provoking prompts to encourage deep exploration and reflection.

However, you may decide to journal separately if the boxes are too restrictive for your process. There are no 'right' or 'wrong' answers to these questions since they are so personal to yourself and life. Whatever thoughts and feelings come up for you, they are valid. Allow your mind and feelings to connect with the paper and see what else comes up for you regarding each topic.

I also refer to empathy at various points in this book. I feel it is important to differentiate between 'empathy' and 'sympathy' as sometimes the terms can understandably get confused. In simplistic terms, empathy involves trying to understand struggles, thoughts and feelings from another person's perspective (Rogers, 1980), whereas sympathy is personally feeling condolences for someone else (Sharma, 1992).

No matter what age or stage of life you are at, there is always room for personal development and self-discovery. We never stop learning. Are you ready to walk along the path towards your ideal, true self? It is lovingly and patiently waiting for you.

Perspective

Although we live in the world together, everyone views it differently, finding their own truth and meaning dependent upon how they perceive and experience it (Sanders, 2006). This is called our phenomenological field.

For example, two people standing side by side observing beautiful scenery may look as if they are having a shared 'moment'. However, each of them will see the apparently same view in a different light. Maybe one person is looking at the birds flying in the air, while the other is admiring the tall oak trees scattered across the landscape. In the same way, we can all look at the same issue or topic yet share different opinions and beliefs on it due to being shaped by our intimate, personal experience of the world.

How we view our self and the world can change over time based upon new experiences we encounter in life, particularly through interactions with others (Rogers, 1951). Previous firmly-held beliefs can melt away, only to be replaced with new ones. Therefore, our self concept and phenomenological field is forever changing to fit our new world view. After all, I am sure many will be able to agree they are not the same person they were a few years ago.

All of our experiences have moulded us into the people we are today. Sometimes relationships may come under strain if perceptions 'clash', and if people find it difficult to take into account how other people may view the exact same situation differently — even scenarios where one may think people will 'obviously' share the same view.

12

Rogers teaches the importance of person-centred therapists remaining curious of their clients' inner world, to really try and understand things from another person's perspective or 'frame of reference' (Rogers, 1957). Whether you agree with another person's perspective or not, this can be attempted by putting one foot in their reality while keeping your other foot firmly planted in your own.

Through mutual respect and an attempt at understanding one another's point of view, newfound insights into how the world looks through another's eyes may be gained, along with relationships possibly being strengthened in the process.

Perspective Questions

In hindsight, what past experiences are you grateful for? How have they moulded you into the person you are today?

- school and having the friendships I have. Made me see how good it can be

- au pairing and my gap year, shaved hair, strong I could be especially the cooking course.

What did you learn from these experiences and in what ways did they shape your perspective?

Think they made me realise how strong I can be and although it was hard at times they allowed me to grow.

Are there any blocks within yourself that stop you from seeing things from other people's perspectives?

Judgement and I think that I know what people are thinking already

14

What can you do to address these blocks?

You can't know what people think. Reminding myself of that.

Change

Rogers believed that people can only change when they accept themselves just as they are (Rogers, 1967). Are you struggling to accept yourself as you are today? Are there things you want to change and develop within yourself but you are unsure how? Accepting oneself just as you are can be easier said than done. What is sometimes difficult to remember is that each part of you serves a purpose and wants the same acceptance as the others... even the parts you perhaps find difficult to acknowledge.

Upon reflection, why are those parts of you there in the first place? What do those parts need in order to set you free to become the person you aspire to be? Is it acceptance as Rogers suggests? Is it tender compassion and love? Whatever it may be, the person-centred approach advocates that everyone has the inherent ability within themselves to reach and realise their full potential, to become their true selves. This is known as self actualisation (Mearns et al., 2013).

If thoughts, beliefs and feelings are pushed down, they are still within you somewhere and are very likely to come back up to the surface — perhaps when you least expect it. It can almost become a vicious cycle if there are parts of yourself you would like to change, but you are not ready to look at them so you push them down... and so the cycle goes on.

16

Maybe you metaphorically feel like your hand is on the doorknob to unlocking the change within yourself, but fear is holding you back from pushing that door open. Are you scared of what you may find lying behind it? Be kind to yourself and if something in you feels ready to push that door open, maybe that room behind the door held the key to the change all along. The key is you.

Change Questions

What part(s) of yourself do you wish to develop?

- critical side
- overthinking
- insecure

What purpose does this part(s) serve within you?

- Keeps me in "control"
- Keeps me safe and along the right lines

What does that part(s) need in order to make the change you wish to see?

- a non judgemental acceptance

Happiness

Are you truly happy? Realistically, your answer to this question may change daily. Rogers believed that happiness or 'the good life' is an ongoing process directed by the individual, rather than a certain destination to be attained (Rogers, 1967).

This makes sense if you think of happiness and other emotions like waves. Waves come and go, sometimes looking fierce and strong, and at other times nonexistent. Therefore happiness in the same way is fleeting and something individuals need to actively seek out.

It has been suggested that expressing gratitude, which can be defined as appreciating what is both meaningful and valuable to you (Sansone & Sansone, 2010), can lead to an increased sense of happiness (Emmons & McCullough, 2003).

However, everyone has the freedom to decide upon which direction to take to move towards their own happiness (Rogers, 1967), finding it from different sources. We are all unique individuals and different things work for different people. After all, no one knows you better than you know yourself — you are the expert of your own life (Rogers, 1959).

It is my hope that you may find the things in life that continue to move you in the direction of seeking out your own happiness daily.

Happiness Questions

What things are you feeling grateful for today?

What things will help you to keep striving to find happiness in your life?

20

Can you identify any blocks in your life today that are stopping you from being happy? If so, what?

- overthinking about things I can't control

What can you do in your life to soften or even remove these blocks entirely?

- being compassionate and allowing myself to let go

Being Yourself

Rogers used the metaphor of everyone being on their own island — one can only build bridges to other islands (e.g. people) if they are both willing and feel permitted to be themselves (Rogers, 1967). Do you feel willing to be your true self today and do you feel 'allowed' to be? I can imagine this is the ideal aspiration a lot of people have — to not be weighed down by hindering aspects stopping this process from happening, to feel you can be wholeheartedly yourself with everyone you meet in life.

Different factors can stop people from being their true self. For instance, everyone has conditions of worth and introjected values. Conditions of worth are conditional responses people receive from others that become part of how they view themselves (Proctor, 2017). For example, these conditions of worth can be identified by thinking of the phrase 'I will only be accepted if...' — something in your life that has a condition attached to it.

Similarly, introjected values are beliefs of others that people absorb to become their own (Lees-Oakes, 2019). For instance, you may say to yourself you 'should' and 'shouldn't' do certain things. However, where did these 'rules' come from? Are they beliefs and values passed down to you from influential people in your life that you have accepted as your own? Or do the 'rules' you have in your life align with your own personal values and how you want to live?

22

These conditions of worth and introjected values can be deeply ingrained in our life, making them difficult to shake. Due to this, you may 'act' a certain way in order to feel like you fit in, but in the process are rejecting your true self if you are being someone you feel you are not. However, being aware of these things can be the first step towards personal growth.

On the flip side, maybe you do things that block other people from being their true self. For example, you may put high expectations on others, trying to mould them into how you want them to be.

By doing this, this may stop people from being able to be their true selves if they are trying to meet the high expectations you place upon them. By being open, curious and accepting of the experiences of others, you are giving people the opportunity to be themselves around you, just like I imagine you wish to be yourself around others.

Being Yourself Questions

What conditions of worth can you identify in your own life?

> *I will only be accepted if...*

Explore if these conditions of worth fit with how you view yourself and the world now.

24

What values and beliefs from others have you taken on to make up your own value system? For example, 'I should do this...' or 'I shouldn't do that...'

Explore if these values and beliefs fit with how you view yourself and the world now.

Are there any things blocking you from being your true self today? If so, what?

What steps could you take to address these things?

26

Are there any things you do that block others from being their true selves? If so, what?

What impact do you think these things have on others?

Making Decisions

Trusting your own decisions, thoughts and judgements can sometimes prove challenging for people. The world may seem a daunting, unsure place to be, and trusting yourself to navigate it may be an even scarier concept.

You may ask yourself things like, how can I trust I am making the 'right' decision? Or, will I always be wondering 'what if' if I do not give something a try and see what happens? Other people can be very firm in their decision-making, perhaps listening to other people's perspectives, but in the end primarily making decisions based on what feels 'right' for them.

We are faced with decisions — some big, others small — on a regular basis, but how we arrive at a conclusion about what decision or direction to take could be very dependent on what is referred to as our locus of evaluation. People use their locus of evaluation to make judgements about others, themselves and the world (Feltham & Dryden, 1993).

Locus of evaluation can be internal or external (Mearns et al., 2013). People with an external locus of evaluation may be more influenced by the opinions of others instead of listening to their own internal experience (Mearns et al., 2013). Therefore people like this are very likely to struggle in making decisions or knowing what they think and feel (Mearns et al., 2013). This may be caused by individuals facing much criticism and judgement from others throughout their life (Mearns et al., 2013).

28

On the other hand, those with an internal locus of evaluation may have received approval and acceptance from others throughout their lives (Mearns et al., 2013). This could lead to them having a stronger sense of self and making decisions more aligned with their true experience (Mearns et al., 2013).

The good news is that people can shift from an external locus of evaluation to a more internal one. This can often happen to clients through the person-centred therapy process by moving to trust their own experience and decision-making (Feltham & Dryden, 1993). I have been humbled to witness this first-hand many times.

In fact, Rogers believed that when clients connect with their internal locus of evaluation, possibly for the first time ever, this is one of the pinnacle moments in therapy for the counsellor (Mearns et al., 2013).

By having an internal locus of evaluation, this is a step towards becoming what Rogers described as a 'fully functioning person' or reaching 'self-actualisation' (Mearns et al., 2013). This means that you trust and access your own internal wisdom held within you instead of looking to find the answer from external sources (Mearns et al., 2013).

Making Decisions Questions 29

What decisions are you faced with today? Discuss.

What things do you usually do before making a final decision about something?

30

Are there any aspects of your decision-making process that you wish to do differently? If so, what and why?

If there are changes you wish to make to your decision-making process, how do you plan to make these changes?

Do you think you have an internal or external locus of evaluation? Discuss.

Self-Worth

Self-worth can be defined as finding personal meaning within your existence along with feelings of fulfilment (Ismail & Tekke, 2015). Caregivers' parenting styles can have a direct impact on a young child's sense of self-worth (Bos et al., 2006). When a child grows older their external environment then plays more of a role in developing their sense of self-worth, such as gaining approval from peers (Bos et al., 2006).

This fits with my observations from both my personal and professional experiences. I believe a sense of self-worth appears to be intertwined with our concept of identity — how we view ourselves in the world and how we think others view us. For example, you may think you are 'known' for certain things you do in society, and these things make up your sense of personal identity. Consequently, you may measure your own self-worth against these external factors such as jobs, people, objects, clubs and societies.

Despite this, people do not stay in a 'fixed' state but instead are ever-evolving (Rogers, 1967), and so too are our life circumstances. External factors — such as those mentioned above — can be swiped away from us, leaving people with feelings of fear, confusion, uncertainty and an overwhelming sense of loss of identity and self-worth. Therefore, if we measure our self-worth against things that are impermanent in nature, it will be built upon shaky foundations, which could easily crumble at any given moment.

In contrast, Rogers said people cope better with failings, challenges and sadness in life, along with being more open with people, if they feel high self-worth (Rogers, 1959). He believed the more aligned a person's view of themselves is with their ideal self, then the more genuine they will be and experience an increased sense of self-worth (Rogers, 1959).

Therefore, this discussion suggests that in order to have a sustainable sense of self-worth, it needs to come from within us rather than from attributing our sense of self-worth to external, impermanent factors in our life. Do you agree?

Self-Worth Questions

What things do you think define your own self-worth?

34

What personal qualities do you pride yourself on?

Is your self-worth intertwined with your sense of identity? Discuss.

Do you think your sense of self-worth at the moment is sustainable if your life circumstances were to change in the future? Discuss.

Relationships

As I am sure many of you will be aware, relationships can be complex and take many different forms. How you are around others may differ depending on the relationship dynamic — be it with your friends, family, acquaintances or romantic partners.

Person-centred therapists are to have three core conditions present within all therapeutic relationships (Rogers, 1957). These are congruence (e.g. being genuine), empathy and unconditional positive regard (e.g. unconditional acceptance) towards their clients (Rogers, 1957).

It is believed therapeutic change can only occur when all these conditions are used at the same time and if both the counsellor and client bring something to the relationship (Sanders, 2006). Rogers said that person-centred therapists are to not only embody these qualities in a professional capacity, but also in all aspects of their lives... it is to be a way of being (Rogers, 1980).

These aspirational qualities not only apply to counsellors but to everyone. Rogers has set the benchmark on which we could strive to build our relationships. Despite this, Rogers' idealistic request to have all three conditions simultaneously present when interacting in various relationships can be, at times, an extremely challenging ask of people. We are only human after all.

For example, maybe you would identify yourself as a 'people pleaser'. If this is the case, you may struggle to be fully congruent within your relationships. Perhaps you do not voice your true opinions and feelings to individuals for fear of hurting their feelings or experiencing potential rejection, and so act to try and keep others happy.

This incongruence does not only apply to the words you say (or do not say, for that matter), but also to your non-verbal communication. You may try and mask your true feelings by smiling when really you are feeling upset or disappointed inside. Perhaps not letting others see your true feelings is a form of self-preservation. However, by denying your experience you deny a part of yourself. Consequently, you are not offering yourself empathy or unconditional positive regard.

Another good example to illustrate the possible difficulty posed on people to instil Rogers' three core conditions is confrontation in relationships. Everyone views confrontation differently depending upon their personal experience with it. Some people may shiver at the mention of the word and automatically go into a flight, fight or freeze response, while others may welcome it.

38

Therefore confrontation could cause a possible barrier for individuals to offer these three core conditions dependent upon the given situation. Nevertheless, if people were able to embody all three core conditions into their 'way of being', it could have an impact on various forms of relationships... for the better.

Relationships Questions

What core conditions do you feel you are best at instilling in your life and relationships? Discuss.

What core conditions do you feel you could work on instilling more in your life and relationships? Discuss.

What relationships in your life would you either like to work on or no longer serve you?

40

What steps could you take to address this?

What does the word 'confrontation' bring up for you?

Why do you think you react to the word 'confrontation' in this way? Discuss.

How will this impact you with regards to being able to offer the three core conditions in your relationships?

Boundaries

Creating boundaries both professionally and personally is extremely important as a way of asserting how you want others to respect you and how you want to respect yourself. For example, counsellors like myself have to maintain professional boundaries in order to ensure ethical practice with clients. This includes making sure all sessions are the same length of time and not socialising with clients outside of sessions (to name a few).

If appropriate and healthy boundaries are not set in your professional and personal life, there will surely be consequences. For example, if you do not set personal boundaries, the impact could be feelings of burnout, or not feeling heard or valued.

You know a personal boundary of yours has been crossed if you feel violated or dismissed in some way — if something feels 'off'. I think a good way of picking up on the sometimes subtle nuances of your personal boundaries being crossed is by listening to your body and 'gut' reaction. We can receive a lot of information about ourselves by listening to our bodies, as emotions involve not only the mind but our heart and gut as well (van der Kolk, 2014).

The brain, heart and gut is in close communication with the vagus nerve, a critical nerve involved in the management and expression of emotions in animals and humans (van der Kolk, 2014). That is why people sometimes describe strong emotions as 'gut-wrenching' — it is all connected.

Therefore being self-aware about what we feel is the first step in discovering why we feel that way (van der Kolk, 2014). If your gut is telling you something does not 'sit well' or feel 'right', there is often a reason for this.

The more you listen to your body and feelings, the more congruent (genuine) you will be to your internal experiencing. In turn you will become more closely aligned with your true self. Let your body and feelings guide you to knowing what boundaries are needed in your life.

I know sometimes setting boundaries can feel extremely daunting — especially if you are maybe not used to having many in your life to date.

However, the longer you delay setting boundaries you would like to have in your life, the longer you delay becoming more aligned with your true self. Being firm and setting boundaries is not selfish or mean, but rather a form of self-respect.

44 Boundaries Questions

What boundaries are you pleased you have set in your life and why?

In what parts of your life (professional or personal) would you like to create boundaries or make existing boundaries stronger?

How do you plan to implement these boundaries in your life?

Discuss what thoughts and feelings were brought up for you when reflecting on the prospect of creating new boundaries or making existing boundaries stronger in your life.

Splits in Self

Sometimes we can be our own worst enemy, feeling torn in two or more separate directions with part of ourselves wanting polar opposite things to the other part(s). This leaves us unsure which side to listen to. Sound familiar?

A contemporary development in person-centred therapy called 'configurations of self' describes this process perfectly (Mearns & Thorne, 2000).

A configuration is a dimension of existence (Mearns et al., 2013), consisting of different parts and sub-personalities within a person (Sanders et al., 2012). Mearns and Thorne suggest that each configuration of self has a different way of experiencing, seeing and behaving in the world (Tolan & Wilkins, 2011).

For example, many of us — if not everyone — will have some sort of 'inner critic', a system of negative attitudes and thoughts (Stinckens et al., 2013). The object of self-criticism can vary greatly from 'who I am' and 'what I do' to 'what I have' (Capaldi & Elliott, 2017).

Perhaps you feel your inner critic is holding you back in life, constantly overshadowing the contrasting things other parts of yourself tell you. This may feel like a never-ending battle for you.

As previously mentioned in the 'Change' topic, each part of you serves a purpose. This includes your inner critic. For instance, maybe your inner critic's voice becomes stronger when it feels the need to protect you in some way due to past experiences you have had, even if that protection is no longer needed?

By shining a different light on your inner critic, being kind to it and empathically looking at what purpose it serves within you, maybe you will be able to understand it more as opposed to possibly resenting it. Then together, by listening, accommodating and respecting what each part of you wants, needs and wishes, maybe your various parts of self can find a way of working together to reach a degree of resolution (Elliott & Greenberg, 2021).

Splits in Self Questions

What splits in yourself can you identify?

48

Looking inward, what does each split within you want, need and wish for?

Discuss how you plan to accommodate and listen to each split in yourself.

Self-Love

Do you struggle to love and appreciate yourself just as you are? As previously mentioned, unconditional positive regard (UPR) e.g. unconditional acceptance is one of the three core conditions needed to bring about therapeutic change, along with congruence (genuineness) and empathy (Sanders, 2006).

However, UPR does not only apply to you showing it to other people — it also applies to you showing it to yourself. It is so easy to focus on things one may view as 'negative', yet ignore anything regarded as positive. A good example of struggling to show UPR to oneself is if someone does not accept or acknowledge compliments from others.

For example, imagine someone were to compliment you on an item of clothing you were wearing. So many people (myself included) are guilty of watering down these compliments, saying things like 'oh, I got it in a sale' instead of just saying 'thank you'... but why?

When other people show their appreciation, why do some people struggle to show that appreciation towards themselves or dismiss the compliment completely? Where is the unconditional love and appreciation you are showing yourself in that moment?

50

Or do you give your time, love and energy so freely to others, yet struggle to give these to yourself? You may pour out everything you have got to others, but one cannot continue to pour from an empty cup. I wonder, what things replenish your cup?

Whatever it may be, replenishing your cup is an act of self-care. Self-care is a way of looking after your health and wellbeing — something that rejuvenates your mind, body and soul. In fact, there is a whole section dedicated to the importance of self-care in the British Association for Counselling and Psychotherapy ethical framework (BACP, 2018). It is not a choice — it is essential.

Although necessary, some people may struggle with showing this vital act of kindness to themselves. Maybe you have to get through a to-do list the length of your arm before you feel you can 'deserve' a rest. If this is the case, it is not an act of self-care. One does not need to earn 'self-care' time if it is essential to your psychological and physical wellbeing.

Despite this, I realise it can be a difficult pattern to break — especially if you are so used to putting the needs of others before your own or feeling you cannot properly take time for yourself if you do not complete certain tasks.

Nevertheless, by not neglecting your mind and body's wants and needs, I believe this to be a form of self-love — and the strongest force in the universe is love (Rogers, 1980). If you believe this to be true, imagine how powerful it would be if you were able to take time for yourself and love yourself unconditionally.

Self-Love Questions

What things do you love most about yourself and why?

What are your strengths?

What self-care activities do you do for yourself?

53

Discuss what parts of yourself you wish to give more love and kindness to today, and how you plan to do that.

Final Thoughts

I hope this little book helped you to learn more about yourself, make connections and unravel that ball of string. This book can be returned to at various stages of your life. Your answers may change to reflect where you are on your personal development journey.

Everyone is capable of change. As my dance teacher used to say, there is no 'I can't do it', but rather 'I find it difficult'. Yes, change can be difficult, but it is not always impossible. This book is not only about changes you wish to see, but also about praising the things you love about yourself. Admirable qualities that you want to carry forth with you for the rest of your life.

Each and every part of you is important. It makes you who you are today and who you aspire to be. I wish you well on life's journey of self-discovery. May you never stop learning and developing, and continue to choose to walk along the path towards your ideal, true self.

References

Baker, N., Cooper, M., Elliott, R., Merry, T., Purton, C., & Worsley, R. (2012). *The Tribes of the Person-Centred Nation*. PCCS Books Ltd.

Bos, A. E. R., Muris, P., Mulkens, S., & Schaalma, H. P. (2006). Changing self-esteem in children and adolescents: A roadmap for future interventions. *Journal of Psychology, 62,* 26-33. DOI: https://psycnet.apa.org/record/2006-21533-006.

British Association for Counselling and Psychotherapy. (2018). *Ethical Framework for the Counselling Professions.* Lutterworth, UK: BACP. Available at: https://www.bacp.co.uk/media/3103/bacp-ethical-framework-for-the-counsellingprofessions-2018.pdf.

Capaldi, K., & Elliott, R. (2017). *Pernicious influences & harmful effects: a discourse analysis of self-critical, self-harming & resulting emotion processes in socially anxious clients.* In School Based Counselling Exhibition, University of Strathclyde. DOI: https://strathprints.strath.ac.uk/75745/.

Cooper, M., O'Hara, M., Schmid, P. F., & Bohart, A. C. (2013). *The Handbook of Person-Centred Psychotherapy and Counselling: Second edition.* Palgrave Macmillan.

Elkins, D. N. (2009). The Medical Model in Psychotherapy: Its Limitations and Failures. *Journal of Humanistic Psychology, 49,* 66-84. DOI: 10.1177/0022167807307901.

Elliott, R., & Greenberg, L. S. (2021). *Emotion-Focused Counselling in Action*. SAGE.

Emmons, R. A., & McCullough, M. E. (2010). Counting Blessings Versus Burdens: An Experimental Investigation of Gratitude and Subjective Well-Being in Daily Life. *Journal of Personality and Social Psychology, 84*(2), 377–389. DOI: 10.1037/0022-3514.84.2.377.

Feltham, C., & Dryden, W. (1993). *Dictionary of Counselling*. Whurr Publishers.

Grice, J. W. (2007). Person-centered structural analyses. In R. W, Robins., R. C., Fraley., & R. F, Krueger (Ed.), *Handbook of research methods in personality psychology* (pp. 557-572). Guilford Press.

Ismail, N. A. H., & Tekke, M. (2015). Rediscovering Rogers's Self Theory and Personality. *Journal of Educational, Health and Community Psychology, 4*(3), 28-36. DOI: 286456614.

Lees-Oakes, R. (2019). Linking Theory to Personal Development [Lecture recording and slides]. Counselling Study Resource: https://student.counsellingtutor.com/courses/linking-theory-to-personal-development/.

Mearns, D., & Thorne, B. (2000). *Person-Centred Therapy Today: New frontiers in theory and practice*. SAGE.

Mearns, D., Thorne, B., & McLeod, J. (2013). *Person-Centred Counselling in Action: 4th Edition.* Sage.

Proctor, C., Tweed, R., & Morris, D. (2016). The Rogerian Fully Functioning Person: A Positive Psychology Perspective. *Journal of Humanistic Psychology, 56*(5), 503–529. DOI: 10.1177/0022167815605936.

Rogers, C. R. (1951). *Client-Centered Therapy.* Constable.

Rogers, C. R. (1957). The necessary and sufficient conditions of therapeutic personality change. *Journal of Consulting Psychology, 21*(2), 95-103. https://doi.org/10.1037/h0045357.

Rogers, C. R. (1959). A theory of therapy, personality and interpersonal relationships as developed in the client-centered framework. In S. Koch (Ed.), *Psychology: A study of a science. Vol. 3:* Formulations of the person and the social context (pp. 184-256). McGraw Hill.

Rogers, C. R. (1967). *On Becoming a Person: A therapist's view of psychotherapy.* Constable and Company Ltd.

Rogers, C. R. (1980). *A Way of Being.* Houghton Mifflin.

Sanders, P. (2006). *The Person-Centred Counselling primer.* PCCS Books Ltd.

Sanders, P., Baker, N., Cooper, M., Elliott, R., Merry, T., Purton, C., & Worsley, R. (2012). *The Tribes of the Person-Centred Nation. An Introduction to the schools of therapy related to the person-centred approach: Second edition.* PCCS Books Ltd.

Sansone, R. A., & Sansone, L. A. (2010). Gratitude and well being: The benefits of appreciation. *Psychiatry, 7*(11), 18–21. DOI: 2010-25532-003.

Sharma, R. M. (1992). Empathy — A Retrospective on its Development in Psychotherapy. *Australian & New Zealand Journal of Psychiatry, 26*(3), 377-390. Doi:10.3109/00048679209072060.

Stinckens, N., Lietaer, G., & Leijssen, M. (2013). Working with the inner critic: Process features and pathways to change. *Person-Centered & Experiential Psychotherapies, 12*(1), 59-78. DOI: 10.1080/14779757.2013.767747.

Tolan, J., & Wilkins, P. (2011). *A person-centred approach to loss and bereavement.* SAGE.

van der Kolk, B. (2014). *The body keeps the score: Mind, brain and body in the transformation of trauma.* Viking Penguin.

Printed in Great Britain
by Amazon